D0480432

CHRISTMAS
RECIPES
The Crafty Way

MICHAEL BARRY

THE ERSKINE PRESS
for JARROLD PUBLISHING

MICHAEL BARRY'S CHRISTMAS RECIPES – THE CRAFTY WAY

Designed and produced by
THE ERSKINE PRESS
Banham, Norwich
for JARROLD PUBLISHING
Whitefriars, Norwich

Recipes by Michael Barry
Food photography by
The Banham Bakehouse, Norfolk
Food Styling by Lesley de Boos
Photographs © Andrew Perkins
Designed by jack afrika Associates

With thanks to the Norwich Food Company Ltd
suppliers of venison and game

Text © Michael Barry 1997
This edition © Jarrold Publishing 1997
ISBN 0-7117-0963-7

Printed in Spain

<u>CONTENTS</u>

INTRODUCTION

Christmas comes but once a year, and that's probably why we need to be reminded how to cook for it each time. We simply forget how many minutes to the pound for a 16 lb turkey, or can we use vegetarian suet in the mince pies because it was twelve months ago since we last had to remember. You will find the answers to those and very many more Christmas cooking questions in this little book. (But in case the answers tantalise you, they are 15 minutes a pound and yes!)

There is, however, rather more than that in these covers. For many of us on the 25th nothing beats turkey, roast potatoes and sprouts. But how about some poached chestnuts in with the sprouts or an effortless way to carve the bird and make gravy? You will find the ideas and recipes here. As with so much of British cooking in the last few years even traditional Christmas food has changed, and not necessarily for the worse. It's always a time for self indulgence, but it is now possible to create a number of the great treats of the season without including all the artery-clogging fats. In fact the fat free Christmas pudding you will find on page 48 together with the fat free mincemeat and the crafty way to roast your turkey can give you a practically fat free Yule without any sacrifice of texture or flavour.

It is not just health that's an issue either. You may find yourself with the need for vegetarian seasonal food. *RELAX!* The meatless dishes developed are just so delicious they may even convert the most carnivorous. Changes in family patterns too, with smaller groups, sometimes with just adults together, give the chance for some more adventurous meals.

I hope I haven't forgotten the cook either. I have gathered together a range of crafty hints to make Christmas easy in the kitchen, a few terrific ideas for the inevitable leftovers, some thoughts on Christmas and New Year parties and even a couple of special preserves you can make in advance to give as presents or enjoy yourselves.

My hope is that this book will help you enjoy your Christmas cooking in new ways: help you enjoy planning and preparing for it both on the page and in the shops; help make things easier in the kitchen on the great day; and not least, help you, your family and friends enjoy the tastiest, healthiest Christmas you have ever had.

Many thanks to Susie Magasiner who for years has helped develop, test, store and retrieve the recipes that make up this book.

A BIT ABOUT VARIETIES OF TURKEY

There are so many kinds of Turkey about these days, a little note of guidance on what their virtues and limitations are would be helpful. Turkey, like chicken, comes in a variety of grades and qualities. Not all of these are mutually exclusive: some of them refer to the breed and some to the method of rearing.

REARING
FREE RANGE: This usually means free access to fresh air and a substantial area of open ground. They're not common and are quite expensive.

TRADITIONAL: Reared in sheds with regular access to daylight and fresh air and some open ground, they're normally allowed to come to maturity quite slowly and are hung for tenderness after being slaughtered. Widely available and moderately expensive.

CONVENTIONAL: Not battery-bred but reared more intensively and in larger units than free range or traditional and normally not hung before processing or freezing – the cheapest.

BREEDS OF TURKEY
BRONZE: A new version of an old-fashioned turkey, this is broad breasted, richly flavoured (some say quite gamey), and black speckled when plucked but not when roasted.

WHITE BREAST: The conventional turkey that we have been used to for some thirty or forty years, very broad breasted and mild in flavour.

NORFOLK BLACK: An ancient breed producing comparatively narrow-breasted turkeys, lighter in weight than modern breeds and with a strongly flavoured and moist flesh.

FRESH v CHILLED v FROZEN
FRESH: There is no doubt from the point of view of flavour and quality that a fresh bird, properly hung before being plucked, produces the best results, but it is more difficult to store and transport and, except amongst specialist butchers or direct from the farm, not always easy to come by.

CHILLED: Chilled birds are widely available and have many of the advantages of fresh ones as they continue to mature in flavour and to tenderize while being chilled.

FROZEN: Frozen turkeys, while in some ways very convenient, lack the flavour or succulence of fresh ones. They are normally frozen immediately after slaughter and have not time to mature either in flavour or tenderness. They are, however, far cheaper than any of the other kinds and if properly defrosted they are perfectly acceptable.

THAWING TIMES FOR FROZEN POULTRY

Frozen poultry must be thawed thoroughly so that it cooks properly. It is best done slowly in the fridge but can be done in cold water. Doing it at room temperature is inadvisable but if you must, make it a cool room.

WEIGHT	THAWING TIME In the fridge 4°C (40°F)	In cold water (hours)
1.4 kg/3 lb	24 hours	8
1.75 kg/4 lb	36 hours	11
2.25 kg/5 lb	42 hours	13
2.7–3.5 kg/6–8 lb	2–2½ days	16–18
3.5–4.5 kg/8–10 lb	2½–2¾ days	18–20
4.5–5.4 kg/10–12 lb	2¾–3 days	20–22
5.4–6.4 kg/12–14 lb	3–3½ days	22–24
6.4–7.3 kg/14–16 lb	3½–3¾ days	24–26
7.3–8.2 kg/16–18 lb	3¾–4 days	26–28
8.2–9 kg/18–20 lb	4–4½ days	28–30

HOW TO REMOVE THE WISHBONE FROM A TURKEY FOR EASY CARVING

Use a very sharp small knife and cut carefully to avoid piercing the skin. Cut the wishbone at the base end near the wing joints first, cut up along the bone to remove from the flesh and loosen at the top, twisting to remove finally. This will vastly facilitate carving.

HOW TO QUICK ROAST A TURKEY

Remove the wishbone as previously described.

Keep the stuffing separate and cook it in a separate baking dish. If you must stuff the bird itself, only stuff the crop or neck end leaving the cavity empty to help even cooking. Half an onion or a cut-up lemon in the cavity provides flavour and moistness. Season both the outside of the bird and the cavity.

Place the prepared bird on a rack in the roasting pan and put 600 ml/1 pint of water under the bird. This will catch the drippings, make gravy and keep the turkey moist as it cooks. (You may need to top up the water as it cooks.)

Cover the breast and legs with butter papers or buttered foil without wrapping it tightly.

Cook it for:
16 minutes per 450 g/1 lb up to 5.5 kg/12 lb in weight
15 minutes per 450 g/1 lb up to 8 kg/18 lb in weight
12 minutes per 450 g/1 lb above 8 kg/18 lb in weight
About 5 minutes longer per 450 g/1 lb for previously frozen birds – but look for instructions on the pack. This weight should be measured after the turkey has been stuffed.

Temperatures: 350–375°F/180–190°C/160°C–170°C Fan/Gas Mark 4–5. Allow the turkey to stand for 20 minutes in a warm place out of the oven before carving.

HOW TO SLOW ROAST A TURKEY

This is an alternative to the conventional roast turkey, cooked over a period of 12 hours or more. Some people believe it makes the cook's life a lot easier on Christmas Day to cook a turkey like this, as all the work is done effectively the day before. An old-fashioned cooker like an Aga with an extremely slow oven is ideal for this, but it can be done at the very lowest setting of modern conventional ovens. A fan oven, however, is not suitable.

Remove the wishbone.

Stuffing: Slow roast turkey can be stuffed in the cavity if you wish. Avoid a meat stuffing. Use a mixture of fresh herbs – parsley, spring onions, celery – with breadcrumbs enriched with butter, bound with an egg and flavoured with the juice and grated rind of a lemon. Any other stuffing mixture you care for – cranberries, chestnuts and mushrooms all are popular flavouring ingredients.

Wrap the turkey thoroughly but loosely with well-buttered greaseproof paper or foil. Do not seal it tightly as it will steam and not roast.

Temperature and oven times: If you have an Aga, the bottom of the simmering oven is the right place. If you have a conventional gas or electric oven, Gas Mark ½, 120°C, 250°F is the right temperature. The cooking time depends to a certain extent on the size of the turkey but for a 5.5–7.3 kg/12–16 lb turkey, 12 hours is a reasonable average. A much smaller bird down to about 4–4.5 kg/9–10 lb may take 9–10 hours, and a much larger bird up to 9 kg/20 lb, may take 13 or 14 hours. It can go in usually around midnight and rest quietly in a switched off oven for about one hour before carving at lunch.

The rest of the meal should be cooked in the conventional way at conventional speeds, especially roast potatoes which do not benefit from long, slow cooking. Either way, make sure the turkey is thoroughly cooked by running a sharp knife or skewer into the thickest part of the thigh where the juices should run absolutely clear. If they don't, the turkey's not cooked yet and needs some more time in the oven. Both these methods produce a very succulent bird which needs to stand for 30 minutes before carving to allow the best texture and moistness to be achieved.

PERFECT HOME-MADE GRAVY

For almost any roast, this is an infallible way of producing perfect gravy. Drain the fat out of the roasting tin. Put 1 tablespoon of flour into the tin and add half a pint of vegetable liquid – either potato, cabbage or from whatever vegetable you are serving. Bring to the boil in the pan, stirring carefully to collect all the lovely bits and add a couple of shakes of Worcestershire sauce. Stir until smooth, then pour through a sieve to catch any little lumps, and there you have it!

TRADITIONAL CHRISTMAS MENUS

WITH TURKEY

Here are some traditional Christmas menus for you to try. All the recipes mentioned are in the book. Of course you can mix and match as your taste and inclinations suggest. You can finish the meals with a Christmas pudding from the selection or one of the more exotic tarts or desserts.

Traditional Christmas lunch

Individual salmon mousse

Turkey with herb stuffing
Herbed sausage patties
Perfect roast potatoes
Roast parsnips
Sprouts with chestnuts
Vichy carrots
Bread sauce
Perfect gravy

An American Thanksgiving or Christmas dinner

Chestnut soup

Turkey with Vermont stuffing
Candied sweet potatoes
Broccoli mimosa
Danish roast potatoes
Cranberry relish
Cranberry sauce

A vegetarian Christmas lunch

Tomato and orange soup

Vegetarian nut Wellington
Potato and celeriac mash
Brussels sprouts Polonaise
Red cabbage and apples

Roast Turkey & Herbed Sausage Patties; Individual Salmon Mousse; Bread Sauce; Perfect Roast Potatoes;
Vichy Carrots & Roast Parsnips; Sprouts with Chestnuts

STUFFINGS

With the turkey ready to cook, the next step to decide is the stuffing. All the best recommendations these days are not to stuff the body cavity, thus allowing the turkey to cook through thoroughly without any danger of the outside being cooked to rags before the centre is safe to eat. Certainly, if you must stuff the cavity, don't do it with a meat stuffing which only adds to the potential hygiene dangers. I've got some delicious stuffings here which you can use in the crop of the bird, that's the breast end, and if you want more stuffing than that will take, you can always pile it into a little dish and bake it alongside the turkey in the last 30–45 minutes of cooking.

FRESH HERB STUFFING

This is a very light and delicate stuffing. If you must stuff the body cavity of a turkey this is the one to do it with.

INGREDIENTS
275 g/10 oz fresh breadcrumbs (white or wholemeal)
100 g/4 oz chopped parsley
1 bunch of spring onions, finely chopped
1 tbsp rubbed thyme (or freeze-dried if not available)
2 tbsp chopped celery leaves
100 g/4 oz butter, at room temperature
2 eggs
Salt and pepper

Mix the breadcrumbs with the herbs and spring onion. Lightly work in the softened butter and stir in the eggs. Season generously. The mixture will be quite loose and soft but will cook to a firm and light stuffing during the roasting process, as the eggs will set it. It has a lovely green fresh texture, very refreshing in the context of a rich Christmas dinner.

VERMONT STUFFING

Every part of America has its own stuffing for turkey used not only at Christmas but for Thanksgiving too. In Florida it would contain citrus, in New Mexico, chilli, in the Mid West, sweetcorn; apples in Oregon and cornbread in Louisiana. The Vermont stuffing comes from New England. It's simple to make and is definitely a firm favourite with my family.

INGREDIENTS
225 g/8 oz dried chestnuts or 350 g/12 oz fresh or vacuum packed chestnuts
225 g/8 oz thick sliced white bread
300 ml/½ pint chicken stock or turkey stock
1 tbsp butter
4 tbsp each chopped onion and celery
½ tsp each black pepper, sage (freeze-dried if possible) and marjoram
1 tsp salt
1 large egg

If using fresh chestnuts, slash them carefully with a knife, dip into boiling water for 35 seconds to a minute, and peel off the outer skin. If using dried chestnuts, soak them overnight. Using fresh water in both cases, simmer the chestnuts for 25 minutes. If using vacuum packed there is no need to soak or cook them first. Chop the chestnuts coarsely.

Cut the bread into cubes. Put it and the chestnuts into a large bowl and pour the chicken stock over. Sauté the onions and celery in the butter and add to the bread mixture. Add the herbs, salt and pepper and stir in the egg. Use to stuff the turkey crop and pile the remaining stuffing into an ovenproof dish to bake.

APRICOT AND PEAR STUFFING FOR A CHRISTMAS GOOSE

This is a delicious stuffing for goose, one that has a lot of the flavours of Middle Europe with dried fruit acting as a counter-balance to the richness of the bird.

INGREDIENTS
100 g/4 oz dried apricots
100 g/4 oz dried pears
150 g/6 oz breadcrumbs
1 bunch spring onions, chopped
2 tbsp chopped parsley
1 pinch of fresh or dried sage
2 eggs
Grated rind and juice of 1 lemon

Soak the apricots and pears overnight in water. Chop them well and mix together with all the other ingredients, and stuff the bird. Follow the recipe for Christmas goose on page 26 for cooking method. Don't forget to weigh the bird after stuffing to calculate the cooking time.

TOMATO AND ORANGE SOUP

A modern soup with a rich yet sharp taste, that is incredibly quick to make. It uses passata, a light purée of Italian tomatoes, sieved and pasteurised with nothing added but a pinch of salt. Additive-free, it provides that rich tomato flavour and colour that are so often missing in English tomatoes. For Cream of Tomato, just add 2 tablespoons of double cream or yoghurt. Serves 4.

INGREDIENTS
1 tbsp olive oil
1 onion, finely chopped
Juice and grated rind of 1 orange
1 x 1 litre/1¾ pint bottle passata
300 ml/½ pint water
Salt and freshly ground black pepper
Cubed tomato to garnish

Heat the oil in a deep pan and add the onion. Cook until translucent and then add the rind and juice of the orange and stir thoroughly. Add the passata and water and bring to the boil. Simmer for not more than 5 minutes. Season to taste and garnish with cubed tomato. This makes a delicious thick soup, but if you prefer you can add more water to thin it down.

GORGONZOLA, PEAR AND WALNUT SALAD

A salad that makes use of the ready prepared salad bags that include a mixture of bitter lettuces, such as frisée (our word frizzy), implying that the leaves are a bit shredded and frilly on the outside. If you can't get hold of a salad bag at the time you want to make the salad, you can make it with any good crisp lettuce or some of the new salad greens like Rocket that are readily available these days. Serves 4.

INGREDIENTS
125 g/5 oz bag mixed salad leaves
100 g/4 oz walnuts, shelled and halved
100 g/4 oz Gorgonzola cheese
1 tsp sugar
½ tsp salt
1 tbsp lemon juice
1 tbsp red wine vinegar
2 tbsp walnut oil
2 tbsp sunflower oil
1 pear, cored and cut into thin slices
Warm crusty bread, to serve

Arrange the salad leaves in a large bowl. Roughly crush three quarters of the walnuts and mix those through the salad leaves. Cut the Gorgonzola into 1 cm/½ in squares and core the pear, toss in the lemon juice and set aside. Sprinkle the salad with the salt and sugar and then the red wine vinegar and toss. Add the walnut oil, the pear and the sunflower oil and toss once again. Do not do this more than 10 minutes before you are ready to eat – it can be done at the very last minute. Sprinkle the salad with the Gorgonzola and serve immediately, decorating with the few remaining pieces of walnuts.

Tomato & Orange Soup; Gorgonzola, Pear & Walnut Salad

PRAWN COCKTAIL

Fashions may come and go but in my book prawn cocktail will always be a favourite. This version is lightly dressed and served on a bed of Rocket, a slightly bitter, peppery leaf that goes so well with the prawns. Serves 4–6.

INGREDIENTS
For the mayonnaise:
1 medium egg
1 tsp Dijon mustard
125 ml/5 fl oz oil (half olive, half sunflower is best)
½ tsp salt
Freshly ground black pepper
Juice and grated rind of a large lime
1 heaped tsp concentrated tomato paste

250 g/9 oz cooked peeled prawns
100 g/4 oz cooked unpeeled Tiger prawns
1 tbsp chopped fresh basil or dill
6–8 Lollo Bianco lettuce leaves
A handful of Rocket leaves (or watercress)

To garnish:
6 slices of lime, sprigs of dill or basil leaves and 6 large unshelled cooked prawns

Make the mayonnaise by hand using a whisk or in a blender.

Whisk the mustard into the egg. Mix the oils and add drop by drop to the egg, whisking all the time. It is essential to add the oil slowly even if using a blender. The mixture should be thick when half the oil is added. Add the grated rind and 1½ tablespoons of the lime juice and whisk again. Season then add the rest of the oil in a thin drizzle. Add the tomato purée and check the seasoning.

NB If the mayonnaise does not thicken it is because the oil has been added too quickly. To rescue, place another yolk into a clean bowl and gradually work in the unthickened mixture drop by drop whisking continuously.

Put the prawns in a bowl, squeeze over the remaining lime juice and stir in the chopped herbs and 3–4 tablespoons of the mayonnaise. Shred the lettuce and Rocket and divide between 6 serving plates or glasses. Pile the prawns on top with a spoonful of the mayonnaise. Garnish with the lime, herbs and unpeeled prawns (the latter look pretty hanging over the rim of a glass).

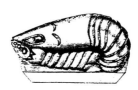

Prawn Cocktail; Smoked Salmon Roulade with Avocado

SMOKED SALMON ROULADE WITH AVOCADO

This is really a very easy dish to make and combines one of the traditional Christmas foods, smoked salmon, with a little lightness and freshness.

For each person you will need:

INGREDIENTS

1 large thin slice of smoked salmon (approx. 50 g/2 oz)	½ ripe avocado
50 g/2 oz cream cheese	Juice of half a lemon
1 tbsp olive oil	Pinch of sugar and salt

1 tsp chopped parsley

Mix together half the lemon juice, the cream cheese and the chopped parsley, and spread the smoked salmon with it. Roll up into a cornet shape and place neatly on a plate. Cut the avocado in half and remove the stone. Peel it carefully using a sharp knife. Put a half face down and cut lengthwise into thin strips without quite severing the pear at the pointed end. Put onto the same plate as the smoked salmon and press gently with the heel of your hand. You will find the pressure will turn each of the avocado halves into a very attractive fan.

Mix the remaining lemon juice with the olive oil, salt and sugar, and pour over the avocado. This should not be kept with the cut avocado for more than half an hour. Keep in the fridge under cling film to maintain its pristine condition.

INDIVIDUAL SALMON MOUSSE

These little mousses are served with a tangy tomato sauce. They are delicious eaten hot, cold or warm and at Christmas time it is good to be flexible. Serves 6.

INGREDIENTS

675 g/1½ lb skinned salmon fillet	100 g/4 fl oz vegetable oil
4 eggs	100 g/4 oz fromage frais (8%)
Juice of half a lemon	Salt and pepper

For the Sauce:

1 clove of garlic	½ tsp each dried basil and thyme
500 ml/18 fl oz passata (sieved puréed tomatoes)	2 tbsp olive oil
2 spring onions	A few fresh basil leaves to garnish

Pre-heat the oven to 325°F/170°C/150°C Fan/Gas Mark 3.

Cut the salmon into chunks, put in a food processor with the oil, eggs, fromage frais, lemon juice and seasoning, and purée it until smooth. Grease 6 individual dariole moulds (or teacups will do fine) thoroughly and line the sides with greaseproof or butter paper. Put the mixture into the moulds and place in a bain-marie (a baking tin half filled with water is ideal) and bake for 20–25 minutes until firm to the touch.

Meanwhile make the tomato sauce. Peel and finely chop the garlic and cook gently in the oil for 2 minutes. Add the passata and the herbs. Season generously and simmer for 10 minutes. Fine chop the trimmed spring onions, add those to the sauce and simmer another 5 minutes. To serve: Put a mousse in the middle of a good sized plate and pour a ladleful of the sauce carefully around it. Garnish with basil leaves.

CHESTNUT SOUP

Chestnut soup is a country house treat. Although chestnuts are commonplace at Christmas in stuffing and with sprouts, although they're eaten on the streets from vendors selling them roasted, there is no tradition outside the 'great houses' of turning them into soup. This is a great pity because they make the most delicious soup, puréed down into a smooth and almost velvety texture. The traditional way was to make it with a game stock from the carcasses of birds from previous meals but in fact I like it as a vegetarian soup. It has a lighter texture and a more delicate flavour. It's also improved served with herb croutons, 5 mm/¼ in cubes of bread fried lightly in olive oil and sprinkled with parsley and thyme before adding to the soup. Serves 6.

INGREDIENTS
450 g/1 lb fresh chestnuts or 225 g/8 oz dried or 350 g/12 oz vacuum packed
30 g/1 oz each olive oil and butter
225 g/8 oz onions, finely chopped
225 g/8 oz potatoes, peeled and cut into 1 cm/½ inch cubes
2 stalks of celery, finely chopped
Small pinch of ground cloves
Salt and pepper
½ tsp oregano

To skin fresh chestnuts: Cut a slit in the base of each of the chestnuts and put into a pan of boiling water for one minute. Take the pan from the heat and remove the chestnuts one by one. You will find the skin, including the brown inner peel, will slip off fairly easily. Remove it from all the chestnuts. If you are using dried chestnuts soak them in warm water for 30 minutes. Discard the water from the pan.

Melt the butter and oil in the pan and add all the vegetables. Turn until coated. Add the chestnuts and turn them as well. Add the cloves, season generously and cover with 900 ml/1½ pints of water. Bring to the boil and simmer for 25 minutes until the chestnuts are cooked through and soft (if using vacuum packed chestnuts you will not need to cook them so long).

Purée the mixture either in a liquidizer or food processor or, if you prefer, through a mouli-legumes. Add the oregano and check for seasoning before serving with the herb croutons.

ROAST PHEASANT WITH APPLES

If you don't have a large number of people to feed at Christmas, or if you just fancy a change from turkey, pheasant is a good alternative. It's got lots of flavour and – as long as it isn't too high – not that greasy a texture. It's easy to cook and has lots of meat on it, unlike duck. A cock pheasant should feed four and a hen two or three. You can, of course, make delicious pheasant casseroles, but I think the festive season needs a festive roast. Make sure it's been properly hung, about 3 days, and do pre-heat the oven: speed is of the essence.

INGREDIENTS
1 pheasant
½ cooking apple, peeled, cored and chopped
1 sprig of thyme
Salt and freshly ground black pepper
Butter paper
1 tbsp redcurrant jelly
1 tbsp double cream

Pre-heat the oven to 425°F/210°C/190°C Fan/Gas Mark 7. Stuff the cleaned pheasant with the apple pieces and thyme. Season the pheasant and place a wrap of butter paper over the top. Put in a casserole and cook for 1 hour (removing the butter paper before the last 10 minutes of cooking).

Take the apple pieces out of the pheasant and put them into a saucepan with the juices from the casserole dish. Add the redcurrant jelly and double cream to the apple mixture. Heat the sauce while stirring until well blended, thick and creamy (you may want to use a blender for smoothness). Place the pheasant on a dish and carefully spoon the sauce around the edges before serving. As an alternative, the sauce can be served in a gravy boat.

Roast Pheasant with Apples

ROAST VENISON WITH GINGER SAUCE

The ingredients in this dish may seem a little outlandish, but the combination of the sweet and sour flavours is ideal with a rich tasting meat like venison. In Germany, the original dish from which the idea comes is called Sauerbrauten and is usually made with a roll of beef like topside, so you can use that instead if you prefer. You will need to plan this dish some time ahead as it needs to marinade for 1–2 days before cooking. Serves 6–8.

INGREDIENTS
2.4 kg/5 lb loin of venison, boned and rolled or a rolled topside
1 bay leaf
1 onion, sliced
1 clove of garlic, crushed
300 ml/½ pint lager
4 tbsp wine or cider vinegar
1 tbsp brown sugar
6 juniper berries
6 allspice berries
6 peppercorns
oil for frying
4–5 gingernut biscuits, crushed

Put the meat into a roasting pan. Make the marinade by putting the bay leaf, sliced onion, garlic, lager and vinegar into a saucepan with the brown sugar and bring to the boil. Meanwhile, crush the juniper and allspice berries and the peppercorns with a pestle and mortar. Put these into the hot marinade, stir and pour over the meat while hot. Leave the meat to marinate for a day or two in a cool place, turning occasionally.

Pre-heat the oven to 350°F/180°C/160°C Fan/Gas Mark 4. Take the meat out of the pan, strain the marinade and reserve. Pat the meat dry with kitchen paper and sauté the joint in a little oil in a large frying pan until browned all over, then place it back in the roasting pan. Pour over the strained marinade, cover the pan with foil, and roast for 20 minutes per 450 g/1 lb. When cooked, transfer the meat to a large serving plate to carve it.

Transfer the roasting juices to a saucepan, bring to the boil, adding a little water if necessary, and add the crushed biscuits. They instantly thicken the liquid, making a rich, glossy sauce. Pour this over the carved meat. Serve with red cabbage and boiled potatoes for a traditional flavour.

Roast Venison with Ginger Sauce; Red Cabbage with Apple

SALMON EN CROUTE

This is perhaps the most popular fish dish I've done. The nice thing about it, is that it comes out looking totally spectacular for remarkably little work. I always use ready-made bought puff pastry which you can get almost everywhere now. This is an impressive dish for dinner parties or buffets. Ask your fishmonger to fillet and skin the fish for you and give you the bones and trimmings for the sauce. Of course you don't have to make two sauces, that's just being flashy! Serves 6–8.

INGREDIENTS

350 g/12 oz white fish (haddock, whiting or cod)	1 tbsp chopped chives
150 g/6 oz fresh white breadcrumbs	1 whole egg
Juice and grated rind of 1 lemon	4 tbsp sunflower oil
1.25 kg/2½ lb salmon, filleted and skinned	1 tbsp chopped parsley
450 g/1 lb puff pastry	Beaten egg, to glaze

Seasoning

For the cucumber sauce:

½ large cucumber	100 g/4 oz fromage frais

For the lemon cream sauce:

Fish trimmings	Juice of half a lemon
4 peppercorns	4 tbsp double cream

Pre-heat the oven to 400°F/200°C/180°C Fan/Gas Mark 6.

Put the white fish, breadcrumbs, lemon juice and rind, herbs, egg and oil into a food processor. Process until smooth. Season well. Roll out the pastry into a long oval shape 15 cm/6 in longer than the salmon fillets and about two and a half times as wide.

Season the salmon and place one fillet in the middle of the pastry, spread with the white fish paste and sandwich with the other salmon fillet. Cut diagonal lines along each side of the puff pastry about 1 cm/½ in apart, leaving 7.5 cm/3 in at each end uncut. Criss-cross the cut strips over each other as if plaiting them over the fish, secure strips with beaten egg. Fold the top flap of pastry into a triangle to make the shape of a fish head and cut a wedge from the bottom flap to make the shape of a tail. Carefully lift the fish on to a greased baking sheet. Brush the pastry with beaten egg and bake for 35–40 minutes.

To see if the fish is cooked, insert a skewer between the plaits; it should come out clean. Serve salmon plain or with either of the following sauces. Cucumber Sauce: Grate the cucumber and sprinkle with salt; leave for 15 minutes to allow the excess water to drain. Rinse and pat dry with kitchen paper. Stir the cucumber into the fromage frais and season. Lemon Cream Sauce: Boil the fish trimmings in a little water along with the lemon juice, bay leaf and peppercorns for 10 minutes. Strain the liquid into a clean pan and boil rapidly until the liquid has reduced to 125 ml/¼ pint. Stir in the cream and season to taste with salt.

Salmon en Croute with Cucumber Sauce

VEGETARIAN NUT WELLINGTON

This is absolutely delicious and rather grand, as it should be for the Christmas feast. It's a completely meat free vegetable mixture wrapped in pastry, and looks as spectacular as it tastes. Serves 4–6.

INGREDIENTS
350 g/12 oz vegetarian puff pastry
1 small onion, peeled and chopped
2 celery sticks
2 garlic cloves, peeled and chopped
2 tbsp sunflower oil
100 g/4 oz walnuts
100 g/4 oz cashew nuts, salted or unsalted
150 g/6 oz chestnut purée (you can buy it in tins)
1 heaped tsp paprika
1 heaped tsp oregano
2 tbsp freshly squeezed lemon juice
Salt and freshly ground black pepper
2 eggs
50 g/2 oz button mushrooms
Beaten egg, to glaze

Pre-heat the oven to 425°F/210°C/190°C Fan/Gas Mark 7.

Roll out the pastry and line a 1 kg/2 lb greased or non-stick loaf tin with it, leaving enough pastry hanging over the edge to fold over and seal in the nut mixture.

Fry the chopped onion, celery and garlic in the oil until the onion is just translucent, then put it into a large bowl. Add the cashew nuts, walnuts, chestnut purée, paprika, oregano, lemon juice and the seasonings, mix it all together and bind it together with the eggs.

Wash the mushrooms by pouring a kettle of boiling water over them in a colander – don't peel them – and put them in a neat pattern in the bottom of the pastry-lined loaf tin (which of course will be the top when you turn it out) and spoon the nut mixture into the tin, patting it down firmly so it fills the spaces between the mushrooms. Brush the pastry you've left hanging over the edge of the tin with the beaten egg, and carefully fold the ends together over the mixture so it is quite covered. Trim the edges and brush the joins with a little more of the beaten egg. Put a baking sheet over the tin and turn it over. Now carefully remove the tin. You now have a perfect loaf-shape without the tin in the way. Cut a little slot in the top and decorate with a few pastry leaves. Brush the top with a little more beaten egg.

Bake for about one hour. Halfway through the cooking time, reduce the temperature to 350°F/180°C/160°C Fan/Gas Mark 4. When it is cooked, the top will be golden and the inside a delight! Serve with the vegetables suggested in my 'vegetarian Christmas' menu on page 8.

Vegetarian Nut Wellington

CHRISTMAS GOOSE WITH SHARP APPLE SAUCE

Though we now think that turkey is the Christmas bird, its dominance is comparatively recent. For centuries geese were the top choice, and now they are making a late-twentieth-century comeback. This is partly because of our considerable appetite for nostalgia, but it is also a sure sign of our rediscovered interest in more complex and mature flavours. Though domestic goose isn't really game, the rich and strong savouriness is closer to that of wild game birds than to the blandness of our modern poultry. This is not likely to be a dish to most children's tastes. Mine certainly prefer turkey, so save it for a Christmas lunch that's for adults only, or for a festive supper over the longer holiday that we see these days. Geese are now widely available both fresh and frozen. Choose one around 2.7–3.2 kg/6–7 lb and expect it to feed about six people. Although when craftily cooked, goose isn't greasy, it is rich. Stuff it with the apricot and pear stuffing and serve with red cabbage and mashed potatoes.

INGREDIENTS
2.7–3.2 kg/6–7 lb goose, well thawed if frozen
Apricot and pear stuffing for Christmas goose (see page 11)
450 g/1 lb Bramley apples, peeled, cored and chopped
30 g/1 oz butter
Pinch of ground cloves
50 g/2 oz sugar

Wash the goose carefully and then place it in a clean sink. Pour a kettle of boiling water over it, turning it half way. Let it drain and then dry for 2 hours. This will help give a crisp skin and prevent greasiness. If you are going to stuff your goose with the apricot and pear stuffing do so now.

Pre-heat the oven to 375°F/190°C/170°C Fan/Gas Mark 5. Place the goose on a rack in a roasting pan and roast for 20 minutes per 450 g/1 lb (remember to weigh the goose once it has been stuffed), plus 20 minutes more. Take the goose out of the oven and leave it to stand for 15 minutes in a warm place.

Don't be tempted to try to turn the fat into gravy. Instead use this sharp, spicy and very traditional sauce. Gently cook the apples with 1 tablespoon water until soft. Add the butter, cloves and sugar, then simmer 15 minutes, until well blended; you can make it sweeter but try it with the goose first.

To carve the goose remember it's easier and safer to carve the breast into three sections a side than attempt delicate slices. The drumsticks, thighs and wings, much smaller than on a turkey, make up the rest of the portions. Don't forget to serve the stuffing – it will have taken on a delicious flavour.

BRUSSELS SPROUTS POLONAISE

Polonaise is just the French culinary term for anything finished in a way they believe Polish food always was, with butter-fried breadcrumbs and chopped hard-boiled egg. In fact, that's exactly the combination that transforms Brussels sprouts into something very special. So special indeed that I often serve this as a vegetable course on its own rather than having it merely as a subordinate dish to meat or fish. It is quite substantial and a revelation for those people for whom sprouts are a burden to be borne every Christmas. Serves 6.

INGREDIENTS
450 g/1 lb small trimmed fresh sprouts　　　　　**50 g/2 oz butter**
100 g/4 oz soft white breadcrumbs (or wholemeal)
2 hard-boiled eggs, shelled and with the whites and yolks separated

Plunge the sprouts into boiling water and cook them for 7–8 minutes until still bright green and firm but cooked through. Drain and run a little cold water over them to stop them going khaki. In a large frying-pan, melt the butter and fry the breadcrumbs quickly until they're light brown. Add the sprouts and allow them to heat through and become partially coated with the breadcrumbs.

Chop the egg whites finely and add those to the pan and pour the mixture into a serving dish, checking for seasoning. Mash the egg yolks with a fork till they're crumbly, sprinkle the yolks over the dish and serve immediately.

SPROUTS AND CHESTNUTS

The most traditionally British way of serving sprouts with turkey. Serves 4.

INGREDIENTS
100 g/4 oz chestnuts (fresh or dried or vacuum packed)　　**50 g/2 oz butter**
450 g/1 lb Brussels sprouts　　　　　　　　　　　　　　**Black pepper**

If you are using dried chestnuts, soak them for 2 hours and then boil them in fresh water for 10 minutes. If you are using fresh chestnuts, first drop them into boiling water for 30 seconds. Then remove them and slit the skins. Replace them in boiling water for a further 30 seconds. Remove them again and they should slip out of their skins. Cook them by simmering in fresh water for 20 minutes; the vacuum packed ones are already cooked.

Meanwhile, boil the sprouts in the normal way; keeping them crisp and light green. Then finely chop them, or purée in a food processor, adding the butter and plenty of black pepper. Serve the purée hot with the cooked chestnuts. The purée has a surprisingly delicate taste and has a lovely fresh green colour.

PERFECT ROAST POTATOES

The secret is in the boiling first. Serves 6–8.

INGREDIENTS
1 kg/2 lb potatoes, King Edwards or Desiree are best　　　**2 tbsp sunflower oil**

Preheat the oven to 375°F/190°C/170°C Fan/Gas Mark 5.

Peel and cut the potatoes into even-sized chunks and place in a pan of salted water. Bring to the boil and simmer for 8 minutes.

Meanwhile, place the oil in a roasting tin large enough to fit all the potatoes comfortably and place in the oven for 5 minutes. Drain the potatoes, remove the roasting tin from the oven and add the potatoes, tossing to coat in the oil. Roast for about 45 minutes, turning once until tender and lightly golden. Serve hot.

DANISH-STYLE ROAST POTATOES

Supercrisp and attractive in appearance these are a terrific alternative way to roast potatoes. Serves 6.

Roast potatoes and roast meat or chicken are perfect partners. Roasting potatoes Danish-style is a bit like icing on a very good cake: it isn't essential, but it's jolly nice! Like all perfect roast potatoes, the secret is to par-boil them first before you roast them in the oven.

INGREDIENTS

675 g/1½ lb potatoes	4 tbsp oil or beef dripping
100–125 g/4–5 oz fresh white breadcrumbs	

Peel the potatoes and make sure they're roughly the same size. Chop any really large ones in half. Put them into a large saucepan of cold, salted water, bring to the boil and let them bubble for 8 minutes. While the potatoes are boiling, put the oil or dripping into a roasting tin and put it in the oven until really hot. When the potatoes have cooked for 8 minutes, drain them well, then slice each one almost through, so there are 5 or 6 cuts in each, like a toast rack.

Take the roasting tin out of the oven and roll each potato in the hot fat. Make sure they end up with the cut surface uppermost and sprinkle each potato with a teaspoon of breadcrumbs. Roast in the top of the oven when you're roasting the meat for at least 45 minutes, basting occasionally with the hot fat. The breadcrumbs turn crispy, they look pretty and add a marvellous crispiness to the potato.

PURÉE OF CELERIAC AND POTATOES

Celeriac is large and knobbly like an aggressive turnip. Its celery flavour though can turn one of our everyday dishes, mashed potato, into a gourmet treat. You can serve the purée with rich foods such as pheasant casserole or rosemary flavoured roast lamb. The almost nutty celeriac flavour comes through strongly but not overwhelmingly. Celeriac, by the way, is mostly available during winter months.

INGREDIENTS

450 g/1 lb celeriac	125 ml/5 fl oz semi-skimmed milk, heated
1 kg/2 lb potatoes	1–2 tbsp fromage frais or butter
Salt and freshly ground black pepper	

Peel the celeriac and potatoes and cut into 2.5 cm/1 inch cubes. Boil together in salted water for 15 minutes. Mash thoroughly and add the heated milk and then the fromage frais or butter. Whisk well until smooth and lightly season.

Vegetables (clockwise from the top) *Purée of Celeriac & Potatoes; Broccoli Mimosa; Candied Sweet Potatoes; Danish Style Roast Potatoes; Brussels Sprouts Polonaise*

BROCCOLI MIMOSA

An extremely pretty way of serving broccoli which is derived from a Chinese recipe that describes the dish with the name of the flowering tree that has the same appearance from its little golden flowers. I have however included it as part of my 'American Christmas' menu as broccoli is so widely eaten in the States. Serves 6–8.

INGREDIENTS

1 hard-boiled egg	675 g/1½ lb broccoli, trimmed and cut into florets
50 g/2 oz butter	100 g/4 oz fresh white breadcrumbs
	Seasoning

Separate the white and yolk of the egg. Finely chop the white and rub the yolk through a sieve and set aside. Cook the broccoli in the usual way in a pan of boiling salted water for 7 minutes until bright emerald green and tender but not at all soggy. Drain it thoroughly and arrange in a serving dish; keep warm. Meanwhile, melt the butter in a frying pan, add the breadcrumbs, season and cook over a low heat until golden brown. Sprinkle over the broccoli and scatter over the egg white and then the yolk to resemble mimosa petals before serving.

CANDIED SWEET POTATOES

Sweet potatoes are a peculiarly American vegetable, although they are now grown all around the world, and are widely available here in ethnic food markets. They are delicious baked in their skins and eaten with butter, salt and pepper; they also make gratins and good soups. But what roast potatoes are to special occasions in Britain, candied sweet potatoes are in the States, especially at Thanksgiving, making it the perfect accompaniment to my 'American Christmas' menu. Serves 4–6

INGREDIENTS

675 g/1½ lb sweet potatoes	2 tbsp soft brown sugar
½ tsp nutmeg	½ tsp cinnamon
	50 g/2 oz butter

Wash the potatoes thoroughly and cut them as necessary to make even-sized pieces. Boil for 20 minutes, drain and peel. Slice the potatoes into 2.5 cm/1 in rounds and lay them in a single, close layer in a baking dish. Sprinkle the sugar and spices over, dot with butter, and grill or bake until the sugar has melted and the topping is bubbling. Served traditionally with turkey, these are good with any plain meat.

VICHY CARROTS

Carrots should not only taste good, but look good too – bright orangey-red to give a lift to the most pedestrian meal. Large carrots tend to be woody with little taste, baby carrots are tender and sweet. Whenever possible, I buy organic carrots, a bit more expensive than the other kind, but well worth it for their sweet, intense flavour. Serves 4–6.

INGREDIENTS

450 g/1 lb carrots, organic for preference	½ tsp salt
1 tsp caster sugar	1 tbsp butter
	A little finely chopped fresh parsley or mint

Peel the carrots and cut them across the grain into slices about 5 mm/¼ in thick. Put them into a medium-sized saucepan so they aren't spread out too thinly – you want them to a depth of about 4 cm/1½ in. Add the salt, sugar, butter and barely cover it all with water. Bring to a rapid boil, turn down and simmer. Cook till all the water has evaporated. The carrots will just be tender and lightly glazed. Sprinkle with the chopped parsley or mint and serve at once so they do not lose that touch of crunchiness.

ROAST PARSNIPS

Roast parsnips seem to be everybody's favourite. In fact, rather like prawns, I find they are one thing I never have enough of. The method of roasting them is, in fact, very similar to the right way to get perfect roast potatoes and involves a little parboiling first. This ensures the insides are cooked soft before the outsides are baked hard so that the pleasure of eating them is not replaced by the problem of entry. Be careful about the timing and make sure when you cut up the parsnips that they have a reasonable amount of bulk; they're not meant to be as thin as chips. If you have tiny parsnips leave them whole: they cook perfectly well this way. Serves 6–8.

INGREDIENTS
675 g/1½ lb parsnips, peeled and cut lengthways   4 tbsp vegetable oil

Pre-heat the oven to 350°F/180°C/160°C Fan/Gas Mark 4.

Parboil the parsnips for 4 minutes, then drain carefully. Place on a hot baking dish with the oil pre-heated in it. Roll the parsnips in the oil and bake for 30 minutes, turning them at least once.

RED CABBAGE WITH APPLES

This is the loveliest way to cook red cabbage and produces a casserole that is purely vegetarian and quite good enough to eat on its own. It's also delicious with game or other rich meats. It can be cooked in advance as it benefits from being gently reheated the next day. Serves 8.

INGREDIENTS

675 g/1½ lb red cabbage	1 cooking apple
1 medium sized onion	1 tbsp cooking oil
2 tbsp cider vinegar	1 tbsp brown sugar

Pinch each of cloves and allspice

Trim the cabbage, peel the onions and core the apple. Cut the cabbage into 1 cm/½ in slices, removing the heavy core. Quarter the apple and cut those crosswise into 5 mm/¼ in slices and halve the onion and cut it likewise.

In an ovenproof casserole, sauté the onion in the oil for a couple of minutes. Add the cabbage and the apple and turn until all have been coated in the oil. Season generously, add the vinegar and brown sugar and a tablespoon or two of water. Put on the lid and cook gently on the top of the stove or in the oven at 325°F/170°C/150°C Fan/Gas Mark 3, for 45–50 minutes. Check that the cabbage isn't drying up about halfway through and stir in the spices.

TURKEY AND WALNUT CROQUETTES

Croquettes are always popular. These are very tasty, very easy and also use up not only the turkey, but all those walnuts that no-one had room for after Christmas lunch! Makes 8.

INGREDIENTS
225 g/8 oz cooked turkey
4 tbsp leftover stuffing
100 g/4 oz shelled walnuts
1 egg, beaten
4 tbsp flour
A little oil

Mince or chop the turkey meat finely – a food processor does this well. Mix thoroughly with the stuffing and the crumbled walnut pieces, then bind with the beaten egg. Shape into little fat sausages about 5 x 2.5 cm/2 x 1 in, roll in the flour and shallow fry gently for about 10 minutes, turning occasionally until brown on all sides. Serve with crisp green cabbage.

POTTED TURKEY

Perfect for post-Christmas use of the inevitable turkey bits. As most people will have had their fill of turkey by the time you get round to making this, why not freeze it? A couple of months later it may prove a revelation which excites praise and smiles instead of groans and head-holding the day after Boxing Day. Serves 4–6.

INGREDIENTS
1 slice of white bread or 2 tbsp stuffing
225 g/8 oz turkey scraps (some with skin will do, though it shouldn't be all skin)
2–3 tbsp giblet stock, gravy or water
½ tsp each salt and freshly ground black pepper
2 tbsp cranberry sauce (if available)
100 g/4 oz butter, melted

Put the bread or stuffing into a food processor or blender and process for 2 or 3 seconds until crumbed. Add the other ingredients, except the butter, and process for about 15 seconds, until a fine purée forms. Scrape down the side of the bowl once or twice. With the motor running, add the butter through the feed tube, until thoroughly blended. Transfer to individual bowls or one large soufflé dish and chill until required. If serving fairly soon, a teaspoon of cranberry sauce piled in the middle with a couple of holly sprigs makes an attractive decoration. Don't freeze it with the holly on though – it won't taste nice and it'll make holes in the cling film!

Potted Turkey; Turkey & Walnut Croquettes

APPLE AND STILTON SOUP

This soup is a great way to use up leftovers from a truckle of Stilton, and it is delicious and sophisticated enough to serve at really quite a smart party. Choose apples with a good flavour such as Cox's rather than Golden Delicious. Serves 6.

INGREDIENTS
1 tbsp oil
30 g/1 oz butter
225 g/8 oz potatoes, diced
225 g/8 oz onion, chopped
450 g/1 lb eating apples, cored but not peeled, diced
1.2 litres/2 pints water
100 g/4 oz blue Stilton
Salt and pepper

Heat the butter in the oil and fry the onion and potato in it for 3 or 4 minutes. Season generously and add the apple chunks and water. Bring to the boil and simmer for 15 minutes till fruit and vegetables are soft. Put into a processor or liquidizer and purée till fine. Add half the cheese and purée again. Season, but go easy on the salt as the rest of the cheese has yet to be added.

Re-heat the mixture and serve in bowls with the remaining cheese, crumbled with a fork, sprinkled on top.

PARSON

An amazing name for a spicy, original dish, dating from the end of the eighteenth century when spices were making their way to Britain from India. It makes a lovely change from plates of turkey salad, and was just the thing to offer the vicar when he came calling after Christmas. Serves 6.

INGREDIENTS
450 g/1 lb rice
1 level tbsp mild curry powder
2 tbsp flour
450 g/1 lb cold cooked turkey, cut into cubes

1 large onion, chopped
2 tbsp butter
600 ml/1 pint milk
2 tbsp olive oil

1–2 tbsp chopped fresh parsley

Boil the rice until cooked. Drain and keep hot. Meanwhile, fry the onion with the curry powder in melted butter for 2 minutes. Stir in the flour and add the milk gradually. Whisk to a smooth sauce. Simmer for 5 minutes then add the turkey and heat through. Grease a ring mould with the olive oil. Sprinkle some chopped parsley on the bottom of the mould and then add the cooked rice. Press it down firmly and cover the mould with a plate. Turn it upside down, give the mould a sharp tap and turn the rice out onto a serving plate. Fill the centre with the Parson and serve immediately.

Parson; Apple & Stilton Soup

CORONATION TURKEY

This particular sauce combination was first invented, as legend has it, for the Coronation dinner of our Queen when, with so many visitors from around the world, it was difficult to produce a meal which could appeal to sophisticated plates and yet conform to the dietary rules dictated by a variety of religions and customs. In its original form the sauce was used with chicken but I think that turkey is an ideal basis for this particularly piquant sauce. It can be made up to 12 hours in advance and kept in the fridge but don't keep it longer than that both for safety's sake and also because it begins to look a little tired. It's a dish that requires piling up high on a pretty plate to make it look good in the middle of a buffet. Serves 8.

INGREDIENTS
225 g/8 oz mayonnaise
225 g/8 oz low fat fromage frais
300 ml/½ pint milk
1 tbsp flour
1 tbsp butter
1 dsp curry powder
Salt and pepper
100 g/4 oz apricot jam
450 g/1 lb leftover turkey off the bone
50 g/2 oz slivered almonds

Melt the butter in a non-stick pan and cook the curry powder gently for 2–3 minutes. Add the flour then the milk and whisk until smooth and thick. Add the jam to the mixture whilst it is still hot and whisk until it melts into the sauce. Leave to cool then stir in the fromage frais and the mayonnaise in turn. Check the sauce for seasoning, it may need a little lemon juice to balance the apricot jam if it's too sweet.

Cut the turkey up into 2.5 cm/1 in cubes and mix thoroughly with the sauce. Toss the slivered almonds in a lightly greased frying pan until they turn pale gold, sprinkle over the top and garnish with parsley or watercress to add a bright green contrast. This is delicious served with the jewelled rice salad on page 44.

BREAD SAUCE

To my family a traditional Christmas feast is not complete without bread sauce. It can be made an hour or so ahead of time. A layer of cling film put directly onto the surface of the dish will prevent a skin from forming. Keep warm in a low oven or by sitting the dish in hot water.

INGREDIENTS

1 large onion, peeled	6 cloves and 6 whole peppercorns
300 ml/½ pint stock	2 bay leaves
A pinch of ground nutmeg	6 slices white bread, crusts removed
300 ml/½ pint full cream milk	1 cinnamon stick

Cut the onion in half and stud both halves with cloves. Put into the stock with the bay leaves and peppercorns and simmer gently for 10–15 minutes until the onion is very soft. Meanwhile crumb the bread. Put the cinnamon and nutmeg into the milk and heat gently. Strain both the stock and the milk into a large clean saucepan and gradually stir in the breadcrumbs. Season well and serve.

CRANBERRY AND ORANGE RELISH

This raw relish is made in moments in a blender, but can be made well in advance of Christmas Day and is wonderfully refreshing.

INGREDIENTS

1 orange, unpeeled – preferable unwaxed and organic	125 g/5 oz sugar
350 g/12 oz frozen cranberries	50 g/2 oz shelled walnuts

Cut the orange into quarters, skin and all, and de-pip. Put the cranberries, walnuts and orange pieces into a blender until roughly chopped but not puréed. Tip half the mixture into a bowl, sprinkle with the sugar, add the rest of the chopped cranberries and mix well. Leave for 2 hours to mature before serving.

OLD FASHIONED CRANBERRY SAUCE

The delicious dark red, cooked sauce that has become a must with our Christmas dinners. Makes 750 g/1½ lb.

INGREDIENTS

225 g/8 oz sugar	225 ml/8 fl oz water
350 g/12 oz cranberries	

Bring the sugar and water to a boil in a heavy-bottomed pan, add the cranberries. When they begin to pop cover with a lid and simmer for 10 minutes. Cool and refrigerate before serving.

HERBED SAUSAGE PATTIES

Serve these around the turkey this year. They will make a welcome change from cocktail sausages or bacon rolls. Serves 8 (makes 16 small patties).

INGREDIENTS

450 g/1 lb good sausage meat – I prefer beef or chicken	1 egg
100 g/4 oz soft white breadcrumbs	1 tbsp flour
1 tsp each marjoram, sage and thyme	1–2 tbsp oil
Salt and freshly ground black pepper	1–2 tbsp oil

Mix together the sausage meat, breadcrumbs, egg, herbs and seasoning. The best way is to plunge in with scrupulously clean hands and knead really thoroughly for two or three minutes. Let the mixture rest for a few minutes. Turn out onto a board and divide into 16 equal pieces. Shape each so it looks a bit like a mini hamburger and coat lightly with flour. Heat the oil in a frying pan and fry for 4–5 minutes on each side until thoroughly cooked through. These are delicious hot or cold.

CUCUMBER AND ORANGE HOLLANDAISE SAUCE

This goes particularly well with baked salmon. Makes about 125 ml/¼ pint.

INGREDIENTS

1 egg	2 egg yolks
Juice of one lemon	½ tsp salt
225 g/8 oz butter, cut into small pieces	Juice of half an orange
¼ cucumber, halved and seeded and cut into fine dice	

Put the egg, egg yolks, lemon juice and salt in a food processor or liquidizer and blend until smooth. Gently heat the butter in a heavy-based, non-stick pan until completely melted and foaming. With the motor running at medium speed, pour the butter onto the egg mixture through the feed tube in a continuous stream – the sauce will amalgamate and thicken almost immediately. Process for another 5 seconds. Pour it out of the food processor back into the hot pan. Stir in the cucumber and orange juice, warm through without allowing to come near the boil, and serve. Keep hot for about 10 minutes over warm water or in a switched-off warm oven.

MULLED CRANBERRY JUICE

This non-alcoholic drink is a spicy winter warmer perfect after a night of carol singing and good for adults and children alike. Cranberries are also packed with Vitamin C, just the thing to keep away chills. This drink can also be strained and served cold, possibly fizzed up with a squirt of soda water. (Makes 6–8 glasses.)

INGREDIENTS

550 ml/18 fl oz cranberry juice	300 ml/½ pint water
300 ml/½ pint freshly squeezed orange juice	Juice of half a lemon
4 allspice berries	4 whole cloves
1 cinnamon stick	A few slices of lemon and orange

Add all the ingredients to a saucepan and slowly bring to the boil. Simmer for 10 minutes to infuse the flavours. Using a slotted spoon remove the spices. Serve with a slice of fruit in each glass.

Clockwise from the top: *Mulled Cranberry Juice; Cranberry & Orange Relish; Herbed Sausage Patties; Cucumber & Orange Hollandaise; Bread Sauce*

BAKED GLAZED SALMON

Whole baked salmon is always a spectacular dish to present, but never more so than in the Christmas and New Year period where a surfeit of meat and fowl always seems to be on offer. Although it used to be fashionable to suggest that only wild salmon will do for this kind of presentation, these days the improved quality of farmed salmon makes them quite delicious and a very affordable treat. Serves 12.

INGREDIENTS
3–3.5 kg/6–7 lb whole salmon
A little sunflower oil
3 limes
300 g/4 oz fine shred lime marmalade
1 tsp Tabasco or chilli sauce

Preheat the oven to 375°F/190°C/170°C Fan/Gas Mark 5/middle of the Aga roasting oven. Have the fishmonger prepare the salmon, or buy it ready-prepared as you can these days from the chill cabinet of a supermarket. You can remove the head if it troubles you but I think the nicest presentation is head on. Lay out a piece of foil double the length of the salmon. Oil the foil and lay the salmon at one end of it. Cut up one of the limes into small pieces and use that to fill the cavity of the salmon. Fold the paper up carefully over the fish and fold into a neat seal without pressing down onto the flesh so that there is an air pocket around the salmon. Lift it carefully onto a baking sheet and bake for 10 minutes per 450 g/1 lb.

Remove from the oven and allow to cool on a flat surface. Remove the foil and very carefully remove the skin from the salmon. You can remove most of the fins at the same time but leave the tail on. Gently melt the lime marmalade with the Tabasco or chilli sauce in a small pan and use this to carefully glaze the salmon with a couple of coats. Slice the limes very thinly and lay these in an attractive pattern along the centre of the salmon, glazing a couple of times more with the lime jelly to set them in. Place the fish on an attractive serving plate, give one last glazing and allow to cool completely. Set for at least 6 hours in the fridge before serving. Serve this as a centrepiece accompanied by the Jewelled rice on page 44 which could be a vegetarian alternative as a main course if the salmon is not acceptable.

Baked Glazed Salmon

TURKEY GALANTINE

This is the centre-piece of the party and can be prepared up to 3 days in advance and kept in the fridge. Serves 15–20 as part of a buffet.

INGREDIENTS

1 boned 4.5–5.4 kg/10–12 lb turkey (get your butcher to do this or try it yourself, practising on a chicken first, you start with a cut along the back of the bird and peel the skin and flesh away from the bones with a very sharp knife, working gently)

2 bunches spring onions

1 red pepper

350 g/12 oz cooked ox tongue

225 g/8 oz fresh breadcrumbs

50 g/ 2 oz shelled pistachio nuts

50 g/ 2 oz crystallized ginger, finely chopped

50 g/ 2 oz fresh parsley, chopped (or 30 g/1 oz freeze-dried)

1 tsp each of ground bay leaves and paprika

1 dsp each of dried thyme and tarragon (freeze-dried for preference)

Salt and pepper

2 eggs, beaten

50 g/2 oz softened butter

Trim and fine chop the spring onions, green and white bits. Trim the red pepper, taking the seeds out carefully, and cut into fine dice. Cut the tongue, which ideally should be in thick slices, into quarter inch dice. Put the breadcrumbs in a bowl and add all the other ingredients except for the eggs and butter and mix thoroughly.

Add the eggs and butter and knead with your hands. Lay the boned turkey out skin side down and put the stuffing in the middle, wrapping the skin round it again as close to the original shape of the bird as possible. Fix with toothpicks or small skewers or, if you prefer, sew up with thin twine.

Place the stuffed turkey on a rack and put the rack in a baking tin. Cover the turkey with butter papers or buttered foil. Put 600 ml/1 pint of water under the rack and bake in a medium oven, 325°F/170°C/150°C Fan/Gas Mark 3, for 15 minutes per 450 g/1 lb (weighing the turkey after it's been stuffed). Switch the oven off and leave to cool completely, this will take about 4 or 5 hours.

Wrap the turkey galantine in greaseproof paper and then in foil or clingfilm and store in the fridge for up to 3 days. You should allow it to get thoroughly cold and chilled, at least 12 hours, before attempting to slice. Cut it across like a loaf of bread in 1–2.5 cm/½–1 in slices which will show the jewelled appearance of the stuffing as well as giving people a share of the turkey meat itself.

Turkey Galantine

JEWELLED RICE SALAD

A salad that is as pretty to look at as its name suggests. Serves 12.

INGREDIENTS

675 g/1½ lb long grain or basmati rice	2 tsp salt
2 large bunches of spring onions, trimmed	4 tbsp olive oil
2 large yellow and 2 large red peppers	100 g/4 oz skinned whole almonds
50 g/2 oz shelled pistachio nuts	50 g/2 oz glacé pineapple
Juice of 2 lemons	

Wash the rice in cold running water until the water runs clear. Put it into a large pan with half the salt, add enough water to go at least 10 cm/4 in above it and bring to the boil. Cook for 8–10 minutes until just cooked through. Drain it well, then pour a jug of cold water through it and drain well again. Transfer to a large serving bowl.

Chop the peppers and the spring onions into fine dice. Put half the olive oil in a frying pan and fry the peppers for 5–10 minutes until softened and add the spring onions and cook for another minute, then add to the rice. In the same pan, fry the almonds and pistachio nuts until lightly golden and add those to the rice mixture with the lemon juice and mix well.

Cut up the glacé pineapple into small pieces and add with the remaining salt and olive oil and mix thoroughly together. The rice should be glistening and should have a jewelled appearance with the red, green, gold and ivory of the vegetables, fruits and nuts dotted through it. Chill until ready to serve.

WINTER VEGETABLE SALAD

This is a very simple salad using ingredients unusual in salad – the root vegetables that are so readily available and at their best at this time of year. We don't think of them as salad vegetables but dressed with a good sharp and well herbed dressing they make a marvellous addition to a buffet. Serves 12.

INGREDIENTS

225 g/8 oz carrots	225 g/8 oz Jerusalem artichokes
1 large potato	2 medium leeks
1 swede	

For the dressing:

4 tbsp olive oil	1 tbsp white wine vinegar
1 tbsp fresh dill, chopped	1 tbsp fresh chives, chopped
Salt and pepper	

Peel the vegetables (except for the leeks, which need to be thoroughly washed), and cut into 1 cm/½ in dice. Steam or boil the vegetables until just cooked and drain. Mix the dressing ingredients together and stir into the hot vegetables. Leave to cool to allow the flavours to develop.

Jewelled Rice Salad; Winter Vegetable Salad

SPICED BEEF

Although we tend now to eat it mostly at Christmas, spiced beef was an ancient way of preserving and flavouring beef to keep it for the winter when refrigeration wasn't available. Don't be tempted to buy a more expensive joint – brisket is, I think, the best of all although silverside does work well. The great trick is to remember to turn the beef every few days and to have the patience to wait until it's fully matured before cooking it. The delicious smell you get from the spicing ingredients is mouth watering long before the beef's ready to be cooked. Serves 30 as part of a buffet.

INGREDIENTS
3.5 kg/8 lb piece rolled brisket or silverside, boned and trimmed
100 g/4 oz soft brown sugar
150 g/6 oz sea salt
40 g/1½ oz black peppercorns
20 g/¾ oz allspice berries
15 g/½ oz cardamom seeds
2 bay leaves, crumbled
300 ml/½ pint hot water

Rub the meat with the sugar and place in a large, glazed pan or pot, not aluminium, in which the meat can lie flat. Cover with a cloth and leave in a cool place for 2 days.

Crush together the sea salt and all the spices (except the bay leaves) in a blender or mortar and pestle, then add the bay leaves. Rub into the meat and leave in a cool place. Turn and baste the beef every 2 days for 12 days, remember to keep the beef cool.

Pre-heat the oven to 250°F/130°C/110°C Fan/Gas Mark ½. Take the meat from the pan and wipe clean. Place in another pan and add the hot water. Cover with layers of foil and put on the lid. Bake in the oven for 6 hours, then remove. When cool, wrap it in greaseproof paper and let it stand for 12 hours. Keep the beef in a cool place at all times. Serve it with chutney and baked potatoes.

CHRISTMAS PUDDINGS

Christmas puddings eaten at this time of year are quite a recent development. As with so many of the Christmas 'traditions' that we currently enjoy, they were introduced by Prince Albert in the nineteenth century. Plum puddings, from which they derive, were eaten widely before but not exclusively at Christmas time, so the coincidence of style and time is not, as one might expect from their taste and flavour, derived from the Medieval period, but from almost living memory. In their original form plum puddings had a great deal of suet in them, a relic of a time when they were made with meat as well, and indeed most modern Christmas puddings still maintain a significant proportion of suet in their mixture. There is a view that this makes for a particularly rich and delicious pudding at a time when self-indulgence is the norm, and there's no question if you want a long matured pudding the traditional kind is best. I've included however an alternative which I've found very popular in recent years which has no suet or indeed any other fat in it at all except for that which occurs naturally in the other ingredients. It's a lighter, moister version with a softer texture but one's that's become for us a firm family favourite.

TRADITIONAL CHRISTMAS PUDDING

This recipe has, so legend recounts, been the Royal Family's favourite Christmas pudding from the time of the first Georges at the beginning of the eighteenth century. It should be made at least 3 weeks before Christmas to allow the flavours to mature. It will keep perfectly well for a year in a cool place. It's very simple and is a very rich grand finale to a Christmas meal. Makes 2 x 675 g/1½ lb puddings.

INGREDIENTS

150 g/6 oz shredded suet	150 g/6 oz soft brown or demerara sugar
150 g/6 oz each seedless raisins and sultanas	150 g/6 oz stoned prunes
150 g/6 oz white self raising flour	100 g/4 oz mixed peel
½ tsp salt	1 tsp mixed spice
½ tsp nutmeg	4 large eggs
150 ml/¼ pint milk	

Mix all the dry ingredients together, beat the milk and eggs until frothy and stir in until thoroughly mixed. Allow to stand in the basin in a cool place, not in the fridge, for 12 hours. Put into pudding basins and cover with a piece of greaseproof paper with a fold in it to allow for the rise. Tie round with string or use a heavyweight elastic band. Cook for 3 hours in a conventional saucepan in 4–5 cm/1½–2 in of water with a lid on, or for an hour and a quarter in a pressure cooker. Check water level from time to time. Allow to cool and store.

Before eating, steam for another hour in a saucepan or 30 minutes in a pressure cooker and serve with any of the conventional accompaniments although this is so rich that a little pouring cream is usually all I prefer.

LOW-FAT CHRISTMAS PUDDING

In the search for the yummy but healthy Christmas, the low-fat Christmas pudding plays an important part. In fact, except for the oils inherent in some of the ingredients (such as the nuts and milk), it's a no-fat pudding, as there is no suet, butter or oil added. It produces a deliciously dark and fruity pudding with the authentic Christmassy taste, but not the leaden weight, of the traditional kind. It responds well to being flamed with rum or brandy and can be re-heated very successfully. What it doesn't take kindly to is long storage. It's mature after a week and unless kept in very dry, cool conditions can develop mould within one month. Best made in December, therefore, ideally a week or two before Christmas and kept in an airtight container. Serves 4–6.

INGREDIENTS
450 g/1 lb wholemeal breadcrumbs
225 g/8 oz currants
225 g/8 oz sultanas
100 g/4 oz apples, grated but not peeled
100 g/4 oz bananas, chopped
100 g/4 oz Brazil nuts, chopped
225 g/ 8 oz soft brown sugar
Juice and rind of 1 lemon
3 tbsp mixed spice
30 g/1 oz almonds, chopped
3 eggs
300 ml/½ pint milk
1 tsp salt

Mix together all the ingredients and stir well. Put the mixture into a greased pudding basin, and cover securely with greaseproof paper. The quantities given make enough for 1 x 2.25 litre/4 pint basin or 2 x 1.2 litre/2 pint basins. Steam for 3 hours and then allow to cool.

Store in a cool, dry place until Christmas Day and then steam for 1 hour, before serving in the traditional way. In a pressure cooker the timings are 1 hour and 25 minutes.

Christmas Pudding

FRUIT AND NUT CHRISTMAS CAKE

To round off the festivities, here is a recipe for a fabulous Christmas cake so full of fruit and nuts there's hardly any room left for cake! It is so rich that it's best made in a ring mould so it can be sliced thinly. Not only does it taste good, but the multi-coloured glacé cherries make it look as though it contains jewels.

INGREDIENTS
125 g/5 oz whole Brazil nuts
125 g/5 oz halved walnuts
125 g/5 oz whole almonds
100 g/4 oz dried apricots
100 g/4 oz chopped dried dates
150 g/6 oz mixed glacé cherries
75 g/3 oz raisins
75 g/3 oz candied peel
Grated rind and juice of 1 lemon
75 g/3 oz sifted plain flour
½ tsp salt
½ tsp baking powder
1 tsp vanilla essence
75 g/3 oz soft brown sugar
3 eggs

Mix all the fruit and nuts together. In a separate large bowl, whisk together all the other ingredients to make a smooth batter. Add the nuts and fruit to the batter and stir well until they are all covered and bound together. Line and grease a 20 cm/8 in cake tin and pour in the cake mixture. Bake for 2 hours at 300°F/150°C/130°C Fan/Gas Mark 2. This cake can be made up to three days before Christmas and will keep for three months in a cake tin.

GILDED MINCE PIES

This way of decorating mince pies goes back to medieval times when the use of very thinly beaten gold leaf was also not unknown in culinary circles. However, this method is not only more suited to our views on what's edible but also a great deal cheaper. Makes 24 mince pies.

INGREDIENTS
450 g/1 lb vegetarian mincemeat (see recipe page 61)
450 g/1 lb ready made puff pastry, thawed if frozen
1 egg yolk
Pinch of saffron powder
Whipped cream, to serve

Fruit & Nut Christmas Cake

Preheat the oven to 400°F/200°C/180°C Fan/Gas Mark 6/top of the Aga roasting oven.

Roll out half the pastry into a thin sheet and stamp out 24 x 7.5 cm/3 in rounds; use to line 24 bun tins. Spoon in the mincemeat to come two-thirds of the way up the bun tins. Roll the remaining half of pastry into another thin sheet and stamp out 24 x 6 cm/2½ in rounds to make lids. Dampen the edges of the filled pastry cases with a little water. Place a lid on each one, fitting them on and cutting a small slot in the top of each one.

Beat the egg yolk with the saffron powder in a small cup. Using a pastry brush, gild the lids with the yolk and saffron mixture and bake the pies for 25 minutes until the pastry is cooked right through and bright gold but not burned! Serve warm or cold with cream.

SAVOURY MINCE PIES

I found this seventeenth century recipe in the records of an old country house. The mince pies are a little bit sweet, but they were actually eaten as a savoury course – they're a bit like a sophisticated sausage roll! I think they are wonderful eaten hot late on Christmas Eve. Makes 20 pies.

INGREDIENTS
675 g/1½ lb shortcrust pastry
225 g/8 oz suet
450 g/1 lb minced beef or lamb
225 g/8 oz Cox's apples, cored and chopped, but not peeled
Juice and grated peel of 1 lemon
½ tsp each ground cloves and mace
2 tbsp caster sugar
1 tsp salt
1 egg, beaten

Pre-heat the oven to 400°F/200°C/180°C Fan/Gas Mark 6.

Roll out the pastry and use to line deep patty tins.

Mix the rest of the ingredients except the egg together. Fill the tarts with the mixture and cover with pastry lids. Brush them with the beaten egg. Bake for 25 to 30 minutes, until brown and cooked through. Serve either hot or cold.

CHOCOLATE AND HAZELNUT TART

This is an extraordinarily pretty pudding that seems to last about 30 seconds after you've put it on the table. Serves 6–8.

INGREDIENTS
100 g/4 oz digestive biscuits
100 g/4 oz whole hazelnuts
75 g/3 oz butter, melted
50 g/2 oz light brown sugar
1 tsp ground cinnamon

For the filling:
125 g/5 oz dark bitter chocolate
75 ml/3 fl oz orange juice
1 x 7 g/¼ oz packet powdered gelatine or Gelazone
3 eggs, separated
225 g/8 oz mascarpone (Italian soft cheese) or any unsalted full fat cream cheese as an alternative
whipped cream, whole toasted hazelnuts or grated bitter chocolate, to decorate

Preheat the oven to 350°F/180°C/160°C Fan/Gas Mark 6.

Put the biscuits and hazelnuts into a food processor and blend until the mixture resembles fine breadcrumbs. Add the melted butter, sugar and cinnamon and mix thoroughly. Use to line the bottom and sides of a 25 cm/10 in loose-bottomed flan tin. Bake for 20 minutes then remove from the oven and leave to cool.

Break the chocolate into small pieces and melt in a heat proof bowl over a pan of hot water. Put the orange juice in a small heavy-based pan and add the gelatine or Gelazone. Stir thoroughly and heat very gently until the gelatine or Gelazone has completely dissolved. Remove from the heat and beat in the melted chocolate and egg yolks. Beat in the mascarpone cheese until the mixture is completely smooth.

Whisk the egg whites in a bowl until they are completely stiff. Fold into the chocolate mixture using a large metal spoon and spoon into the cooled biscuit case. Spread until the top is smooth and chill for at least 4 hours. You can decorate with whipped cream, whole toasted hazelnuts or grated bitter chocolate.

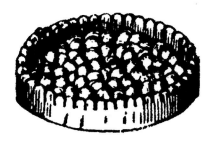

CHOCOLATE AND CHESTNUT ROULADE

This all time favourite makes a sophisticated and festive end to a dinner party. Here I have suggested a chestnut cream filling, but once the technique of making a roulade has been mastered you could make all kinds of variations. Chopped fresh fruit, candied peel, chocolate shavings, all manner of flavourings can be added to the cream filling. Do buy good quality chocolate, look for a brand with at least 50% cocoa solids, it makes all the difference. The roulade needs to cool in the tin for 8 hours after cooking so this is best started the day before you plan to serve it. Serves 6–8.

INGREDIENTS
150 g/6 oz plain dark chocolate, not cake covering
2 tbsp water
5 eggs, separated
6 oz caster sugar

For the filling:
175 ml/6 fl oz whipping cream
100–125 g/3–4 ozs chestnut purée
2 marron glacé, chopped (optional)
2 tsp caster sugar to sweeten or to taste
A few drops of rum flavouring (optional)
Icing sugar to dust

Pre-heat the oven to 375°F/190°C/170°C Fan/Gas Mark 5.

Line the bottom and sides of a 32 x 23 cm/13 x 9 in Swiss roll tin with baking parchment. Melt the chocolate and water together over a gentle heat. Whisk the egg yolks and sugar together until thick, pale and mousse-like. Gently fold in the chocolate.

With a clean, dry whisk, beat the egg whites until stiff, then fold into the chocolate mixture. Pour into the prepared tin and smooth to the edges. Bake for 15–20 minutes. The surface will have risen and have a crust. Gently press the centre to make sure it is cooked. Remove from the oven and cover with a sheet of baking parchment and a tea towel, leave to cool in the tin for at least 8 hours.

Uncover the roulade, laying the baking parchment onto the tea towel, carefully invert the roulade onto this and peel away the lining paper. Trim the edges using a sharp knife. To make the filling, whip the cream until thick. Mash the chestnut purée together with the sugar and rum flavouring. Fold into the cream. Stir in the marron glacé and taste for sweetness. Spread with the cream. Roll the roulade lengthways, using the parchment to help you. It is the nature of a roulade to crack. Carefully lift onto a plate and dust with icing sugar. You can decorate with whipped cream or chocolate flakes if you wish. This dessert can also be frozen quite successfully.

Chocolate & Hazelnut Tart; Chocolate & Chestnut Roulade

CHRISTMAS PYRAMID

You can kill two birds with one stone with this amazing dessert. It doubles as an impressive centrepiece for the table. Also, after possibly overdoing the main course, you can help yourself when you like. Don't be afraid to decorate it flamboyantly – Christmas baubles, ribbon, even cake candles on the top – although don't forget to remove them before you tuck in. And, if you're short on time or effort, you can buy the meringues, although home-made ones will keep in an airtight container for up to a week. Serves 6–8.

INGREDIENTS
8 egg whites
450 g/1 lb caster sugar

For the filling:
600 ml/1 pint double cream or 450 ml/¾ pint double cream and 150 ml/¼ pint yoghurt
1 tbsp instant coffee (or to taste)
2 tbsp boiling water

Pre-heat the oven to 225°F/110°C/90°C Fan/Gas Mark ¼.

Whisk the egg whites until stiff; then gradually whisk in half the sugar and fold in the remainder. Pipe or place dessertspoonfuls of the mixture on to lightly greased greaseproof paper on a baking tray and bake for 1½–2 hours or until the meringues have dried out. Carefully remove from the paper and leave until cold. It should make about 30 meringues.

To make the filling, whisk the cream until thick. If using cream and yoghurt, whisk the cream first and then mix with the yoghurt. Dissolve the coffee in boiling water. Leave until cool and them mix into the cream. Sandwich pairs of meringues with a dessertspoon of filling and pile on a dish in a pyramid. Decorate.

Christmas Pyramid

MINCE PIE ROYALE

By common consent, this is the most spectacular-looking and tasting mince pie, topped with a sticky golden meringue! You can make it as individual mince pies instead of one large one, in which case reduce the cooking time by a third. Serves 6.

INGREDIENTS

225 g/8 oz good shortcrust pastry

225 g/8 oz mincemeat (see recipe on page 61)

1 tsp cider or white wine vinegar (NOT malt vinegar)

Juice and grated rind of 1 orange

2 egg whites

100 g/4 oz caster sugar

Pre-heat the oven to 400°F/200°C/180°C Fan/Gas Mark 6.

Grease a 20 cm/8 in flan tin. Roll out the pastry and line the flan tin with it. Prick the pastry with a fork and bake blind for 10–15 minutes until it turns a pale gold. Remove and let it cool.

In a bowl, mix together the mincemeat and grated rind and juice of the orange, then spoon it into the flan case. Whip the egg whites until thick and add the sugar a spoonful at a time, whipping until the meringue is beautifully glossy. Stir in the teaspoon of cider or white wine vinegar. This turns the mixture into an Italian-style meringue that is crisp on the outside and slightly chewy and marshmallowy in the centre. Pile the meringue mixture on to the mincemeat, swirling it round with the back of a spoon until the pie is completely covered and the meringue is in attractive peaks.

Bake in the same temperature oven for 25 minutes. The meringue topping will turn gold and crisp – but do keep an eye on it, you should not let it go brown or burnt. Allow the pie to cool before removing it from the tin and serving as a very spectacular and succulent pudding.

REAL EGG CUSTARD

To put the finishing touch to your puddings, serve them with custard, that great British favourite. But real custard is slightly paler than the imitation, slightly less sweet, and infinitely more delicious. Serves 4–6.

INGREDIENTS

3 egg yolks

1 tsp cornflour

2 dsp caster sugar

1 tsp vanilla essence

300ml/½ pint milk

Whisk the egg yolks, sugar, cornflour and vanilla essence. Gently heat the milk, and add to the other ingredients. Whisk and pour into a saucepan. Simmer the custard gently stirring continuously, until thickened. Custard can be kept warm for half and hour by placing a jug of it in a pan of hot water and covering the surface with cling film to stop a skin forming. It can be served cold if you prefer.

Mince Pie Royale

WALNUT BREAD

The French bake wonderful bread, with a huge variety of textures and tastes. One of my favourites is this walnut bread from the South-west. It is a small, chewy loaf, often with a dark brown crust and richly studded with walnuts. The slightly sweet and chewy texture goes marvellously with cheese, and it is also a delight eaten on its own, with just a little good butter. This recipe makes two medium-sized loaves which will keep for four or five days. Once they have completely cooled, keep them loosely wrapped in a plastic bag.

INGREDIENTS
1 tbsp soft dark brown sugar
30 g/1 oz fresh yeast
450 ml/15 fl oz warm water
350 g/12 oz unbleached strong white bread flour
350 g/12 oz wholemeal bread flour
½ tsp salt
3 tbsp walnut oil
100 g/4 oz shelled walnuts

Pre-heat the oven to 425°F/220°C/200°C Fan/Gas Mark 7.

Put the yeast in a bowl and add just a pinch of the sugar and 100 ml/4 fl oz of the warm water. Stir until thoroughly blended, then leave for 10 minutes until frothy.

Mix the white and wholemeal flours together and add the salt and walnut oil. When the yeast has frothed, add it to the flour with most of the remaining warm water and knead together until you have a resilient, elastic dough. Don't add all the water, keep a little back and see how much water the flour will absorb.

Put the dough aside to rise in a warm place under a cloth for 45–50 minutes. It should comfortably double in size. Knock it down with the back of your hand and knead again briefly, adding the rest of the sugar and three-quarters of the walnuts which you can crush lightly in your hand as you knead.

Divide the dough in two and shape into two large rolls or cushion shapes, or you can put them into two greased 450 g/1 lb loaf tins. Stud the loaves with the remaining walnuts and put to rise on a baking tray in a warm place covered with a cloth for 30–40 minutes until fully risen. Bake the loaves for 25 minutes, then reduce the temperature to 350°F/180°C/170°C Fan/Gas Mark 4, and bake for another 20–25 minutes until the bottom sounds hollow when you tap it. Remove to a wire rack and allow to cool completely before slicing and eating.

HOME MADE VEGETARIAN MINCEMEAT

Not a traditional method of making micemeat, but with all the old style rich flavours – and no fat! It is not the sort of mincemeat that keeps for months and is best made in the days running up to Christmas. It will however keep for a week or so in the fridge. Makes 1.5 kg/3 lb mincemeat.

INGREDIENTS
450 g/1 lb cooking apples
225 ml/8 fl oz freshly pressed apple juice
225 g/8 oz each sultanas, currants and raisins
50 g/2 oz butter
½ tsp each ground cloves, cinnamon and ground nutmeg
50 g/2 oz light soft brown sugar
50 g/2 oz pecan nut halves
100 g/4 oz slivered almonds

Peel and core the apples, cut them into walnut-sized pieces and place in a pan with the apple juice. Cook for 5–10 minutes until they start to dissolve. Add the fruit, butter, spices and sugar and simmer over a very low heat for 20 minutes. If the mixture starts to dry out, add a little more water to keep it moist but not runny. Add the nuts and cook very gently for another 5 minutes. Stir thoroughly to prevent it sticking and allow it to cool. Cover and chill until needed. It is now ready to be used for mince pies.

CHRISTMAS PRESERVE

This festive preserve is packed with seasonal goodies: pinenuts, crystallized ginger, figs, sultanas. It keeps well, and the flavours mature with time. It would make an ideal Christmas gift. (Makes approx. 1.5 kg/3 lb.)

INGREDIENTS

3 navel oranges	1 lemon
3 litres/5¼ pints water	2.4 kg/5 lb preserving sugar
100 g/4 oz pinenuts	225 g/8 oz sultanas
225 g/8 oz dried figs, chopped	100 g/4 oz crystallized ginger, chopped

Cut the oranges into quarters, remove the seeds and slice thinly. Halve the lemons, removing the seeds, slice thinly and put them into a large saucepan with the oranges and water and bring to the boil. Simmer uncovered for about 1 hour until the peels are soft.

Warm the sugar in the oven, then add to the fruit, stirring until dissolved. Toast the pinenuts in a dry frying pan for 2 to 3 minutes until golden and add to the pan with the rest of the ingredients. Boil rapidly, uncovered, until setting point is reached. This will take about 40 minutes. Remove the pan from the heat and leave to stand for 10 minutes. Stir to distribute the fruit and pour into warm, sterilized jars. You may need to stir the preserve in the jars again to stop the fruit sinking. When cool, cover and seal.

SPICED KUMQUATS

Here is a preserve meant to be eaten with cold meats or cheese. It's made from the baby oranges known as kumquats which can be eaten whole, skin and all. It's a process that, adjusted for the ingredient, can be used with a variety of soft fruits to make spectacular spiced pickles. Makes about 1 kg/2 lb.

INGREDIENTS

1 kg/2 lb kumquats	150 g/6 oz caster sugar
2 tbsp white wine or cider vinegar	4 star anise
10 coriander seeds	2 bay leaves
1 dried red chilli pepper	6 peppercorns

Place the kumquats in a stainless steel or non-stick pan, cover them with water and bring to the boil. Strain and discard the water, put the fruit back in the pan, and add enough water to come just below the surface of the fruit. Simmer gently for 35 minutes or so until the fruit is becoming translucent.

Remove the pan from the heat, add the sugar and wine or cider vinegar to the liquid and stir continuously until the sugar dissolves. Bring the whole thing to a rolling boil for about 5 minutes.

Take out the fruit and place in sterilized jars with the star anise, coriander seeds, bay leaves, chilli pepper and peppercorns divided up between them. Top up with the liquid until the jar is completely full. Cover but don't seal down tight until the fruit is cold.

CHOCOLATE TRUFFLES

These are perfect with coffee after a dinner party, sheer self-indulgence any time of the year, but particularly wonderful at Christmas. Make them the week before and hide them in the fridge – if you don't, they will instantly vanish! They are better than anything you can buy, and cheap to make. Makes approx. 400 g/14 oz.

INGREDIENTS

350 g/12 oz plain chocolate	30 g/1 oz unsalted butter
30 g/1 oz ground almonds	2 tbsp double cream
Grated rind of an orange	3 egg yolks

Possible coatings are 2 tbsp of any of the following:
cocoa powder, icing sugar, ground almonds or chocolate Hundreds and Thousands

Put all the truffle ingredients except the yolks into a saucepan and heat gently, stirring until the mixture has blended into a smooth consistency. Remove from the heat, beat in the yolks, pour onto a plate and place in the fridge for 1 hour.

Sprinkle whichever of the coatings you have chosen into a Swiss roll tin. Remove the chocolate mixture from the fridge after 1 hour, scoop up a teaspoonful and roll it into a ball. Repeat until you have used up (or eaten) all the chocolate, then roll each ball thoroughly in the coating. Place the chocolates in paper casings and chill for at least 1 hour before eating. Best within 4–5 days.

m the top: *Home-made Vegetarian Mincemeat; Spiced Kumquats; Christmas Preserve; Chocolate Truffles*

INDEX

Numbers in italics refer to illustrations